Stanley Matthews

Speech of Stanley Matthews of Athens, Ohio, August 25, 1877

On Political Questions

Stanley Matthews

Speech of Stanley Matthews of Athens, Ohio, August 25, 1877
On Political Questions

ISBN/EAN: 9783337080723

Printed in Europe, USA, Canada, Australia, Japan

Cover: Foto ©Suzi / pixelio.de

More available books at **www.hansebooks.com**

SPEECH

OF

STANLEY MATTHEWS

AT ATHENS, OHIO,

AUGUST 25, 1877,

ON POLITICAL QUESTIONS.

CINCINNATI:
ROBERT CLARKE & CO., PRINTERS
1877.

SPEECH

OF

STANLEY MATTHEWS

AT ATHENS, OHIO,

AUGUST 25, 1877,

ON POLITICAL QUESTIONS.

CINCINNATI:
ROBERT CLARKE & CO., PRINTERS.
1877.

Fellow-Citizens :

The present political contest in this State opens upon its people in circumstances of unusual interest, and opens to discussion many questions of unusual gravity. Some of them are invested with the attraction of novelty ; some of them, if not altogether new, acquire new importance in consequence of new relations and new applications ; some are more familiar, but not, on that account, trite and hackneyed, while others require us to consider the administraration of our Governments, State and National—not in the aspect of party interests and divisions, but penetrating below the surface of ordinary political debate, to explore principles which lie at the foundation of government itself, the explanation of which is to be sought in the solutions of social philosophy.

Let it not be said that themes so profound and momentous are unfit for popular discussion ; that such issues are incapable of settlement by the popular judgment. The human mind is master of human destiny. The necessity of thought and action is upon the race. There is no tribunal but human reason for the solution of the problems of life, and it is the educated reason of mankind which corrects by cancellation the aberrations of conflicting and contradictory interests adverse to truth, and which constitutes *the philosophy of common sense*, that harnesses together, in equal speed, the original and divine wisdom of individual genius and the acquired wisdom of common experience, and drives the triumphant chariot of human progress, with smoking wheels, to the goal of a perfected social life. To this end human governments exist and are administered ; to this end are civil freedom and public liberty developed and established in republican institutions, based on universal suffrage ; to this end are the generous rivalry and healthy strife of political parties, however tainted for the time with sordid, mean, and dishonorable passions ; to

(3)

this end, that righteousness and peace may possess the people and rule the land !

The chief topics thus brought forward for discussion, either by ourselves or our political opponents, may be stated as follows :

1. The Presidential Title, charged by the Democratic party to have been acquired by Republican frauds, and exercised without moral right.

2. The Southern Policy of the Administration, as manifested in its failure to recognize and refusal to support by military force the claims of the so-called Chamberlain and Packard State Governments in South Carolina and Louisiana respectively.

3. The principles of the reform of the Civil Service, divorcing the official influence of the Federal Government from the management of party politics.

4. The reform of the Currency by a resumption of specie payments through the remonetization of silver.

5. The reconciliation of the claims of Property and of Labor by protecting the rights of both, and harmonizing their interests, so far as that can be promoted, by legitimate and constitutional exertions of the powers of Government, State and National.

Fortunately the Republican party is accustomed to deal with questions both new and large. No issues so mighty, so difficult, so fraught with weal or woe, have ever been conducted to more successful and prosperous results than those with which it has been charged. Born of the sentiment which looked upon negro slavery as a reproach to our name, a blot upon our institutions, and a burden to our prosperity, it organized itself to protect the Constitution against its encroachments. Its advent to power as a political party was resisted by war against the integrity of the Union. By war it maintained the indestructibility of the Union, and awoke in the hearts of the people the vivid consciousness that we are a Nation, one and indivisible. It overthrew the institution of American slavery, as the sole cause of sectional divisions, the one standing threat against our peace, and converted four millions of slaves into freemen; and for their self-protection and the means of their political education, incorporated them into the body politic as citizens, upon the broad ground of the equality of all men, as such, before the law. It has restored to their proper relations in the Union the reconstructed States, equal in all respects with their sister states, sharing in just proportions the burdens and the benefits of self-government. It has reconciled the principles of the Declaration of Independence with the Federal Constitution, and in this fundamental law has adjusted the true theory of the rights of men, the autonomy of the States, and the authority of the Nation. The same justice which it has introduced into the relations of its members and constituents at home, it has practiced in its intercourse with the community of nations, and established on a firm and lasting footing our peace abroad, securing the respect and good will of all the world.

Struggling under the load of a colossal debt, we have strengthened our public credit by a conscientious and punctilious observance of good faith in our dealings with our creditors, and have introduced among ourselves a National Money, which, when placed upon a permanent basis, and adjusted with the gold and silver standards of the world, is destined to realize the dreams of political economists of a perfect currency. We have addressed ourselves with diligence and earnestness to the improvement of the machinery of civil administration and the purification of party politics, opening the way more perfectly for the original and independent action of the people in their primary assemblies, in shaping the political conduct of public affairs, so that, through a pure civil service, we may realize the ideal—of a government *of* the people, *by* the people, *for* the people.

The great mission of the Republican party has been to educate the people in the great ideas which are the living source of social and political progress. Its most difficult task has been to educate that portion of the people that naturally belong to the Democratic party. And yet, even here, its labors have not been without fruit, and it has met

with most encouraging success. In 1860, it turned them
out of power and place. In 1865, it convinced them that
the war for the Union was not a failure. It reconciled
them to the abolition of slavery, and, after incorporating
universal freedom and equal suffrage into the amended
Constitution, induced them to incorporate them into the
Democratic platform; so that while the Republican party
pursued the line of march from one reform to another, the
Democrats have followed at respectful distance, bivouack-
ing each night in our deserted camps, hanging on our rear,
and picking up our stragglers, sore-footed and sore-headed
—its only victories, its only trophies, and its only recruits.

And now, the Republican party having settled the great
questions of Secession, of the Civil War, of Emancipation,
of Equal Suffrage and Citizenship, of Nationality, of Re-
construction, of State Self-Government, of the Public Debt
and Credit, laid the foundations of the National Currency
of the future, begun the great work of Civil Reform,
moves on, without fear, to the other and perhaps greater
questions now rising for debate and decision. It will meet
them, I believe, with courage, and solve them with success.
It will still pursue with confidence the paths of progress
and of peace, under its broad and ancient banner—Equal
and exact justice to all men—until it answers to the description given of the model American Statesman and
Hero—the great Washington—first in War, first in Peace,
first in the hearts of its Countrymen.

THE PRESIDENTIAL TITLE.

The instances in our political history have been rare, indeed, in which there was any question as to the integrity
of a Presidential election. We have been happily free
from that which has been too often the plague and torment
of countries in which the title to Executive power is determined by the law of hereditary succession, and where dis-
putes of dynasties have plunged the hapless people into the
miseries and anarchy of civil war. Respectful submission
to the result of free and fair election, declared according to
the forms of law, by duly constituted authorities, is the law

of our well-being, as it is the very spirit of republican institutions, and has, in general, been that habit of the American people, which marked their special fitness for free self-government.

And yet our own experience is not without its warnings, as it has not been without its perils and its trials.

In the very beginning of the century—in 1800—the Presidency became the subject of an intrigue, by which Burr, having received, on the same ticket with Jefferson, an equal number of electoral votes, without a designation of either, as the Constitution then stood, to the offices of President and Vice-President, sought to defeat the known preference of the electoral body. The election devolved on the House of Representatives, which was so evenly divided as to put the result into great doubt. Nothing but the firm and clear-sighted patriotism of Alexander Hamilton averted the danger, whose magnitude none so well as he comprehended. He paid the penalty for this eminent public service with his life : for it is not doubtful that this was the mortal offense which, four years later, he expiated on the bloody field of Hoboken.

Afterward, in 1824, the Presidential choice devolved again on the House of Representatives. Jackson had received the highest number of electoral votes, but was defeated by a coalition between Adams and Clay. Adams became President, and Clay, Secretary of State. The result was regarded by General Jackson and his friends as proof of the " bargain, intrigue, and corruption," which, in 1828, was the staple accusation against the party of Adams and Clay, and which pursued them both for many years after. The sober judgment of even contemporary history exonerated these distinguished men from the charge of dishonorable intrigue ; but the Jackson Democracy asserted and believed it quite as honestly, to say the least, as the Tilden-Adams Democracy of to-day imputes alleged wrong to President Hayes. The good name of a public man is the property of the Commonwealth. He who slanders it defames himself and impeaches his own credibility.

In 1861, the Democratic party rent asunder the Union

rather than peaceably submit to the inauguration of a Republican President. There was no question as to the fact
or rightfulness of his election; but it was made the pretext and signal for a disruption. The Democratic party
had taught itself to believe that it was the exclusive depos-
itary of some divine right to rule; and the election of Mr.
Lincoln, though constitutional in itself, rudely shocked the
party tradition of infallibility. He was treated as an in-
truder and a trespasser whom it was lawful to eject and
expel. There was not then, as now, the same solicitude
that the public will, as expressed through constitutional
forms, should be accepted and obeyed; and it is to be
hoped that some part of the concern now manifested by
the Democratic party in that behalf is dictated by remorse
on account of the attempt heretofore made, in its name, to
defeat the adverse choice of the people. Neither should it
be forgotten in this connection, that it was the license of
rude and malevolent speech, born of the malice of party
disappointment, that hatched its wicked progeny in the
brain of Wilkes Booth, and introduced for the first time
in our politics the example of assassination as an instrument of party success.

The slander of the Presidential title would seem to be
altogether inconsequential; and yet it seems to be indulged
in with gravity by antiquated Democrats, who mistake
themselves for saints, when they are merely mummies; and
spots the columns of fly-blown newspapers, in paragraphs
pointed with malice, which they confound with wit. The
authority and dignity of the Presidential office are gath-
ered, like robes of State, upon the person of Rutherford
B. Hayes; and worthily he wears them! He sits in the
chair of the Chief Magistracy, supported by the law of
the land and the voice of the people; calm and compla-
cent in the conscious possession of the public respect and
affection; caring far less for his personal place, either in
power or in history, than that he should administer his
high trust with wisdom, and deserve well of the country
he seeks to benefit and serve. It is nothing to him certainly—quite as little to any one else, perhaps—that there

be some too dainty to meet the warmth of his grasp with
an ungloved hand—that the Joshua of the Manhattan Club
bids the sun to stop, and the planet to cease revolving,
until Cronin's vote is counted—that clowns and harlequins,
in paint and feathers, the mock savages of St. Tammany,
brandishing war clubs stuffed with saw-dust, with " long
talks " of *de jure* and *de facto*, magnify the *wampum* they
might have captured, if their *braves* had not all proved to
have been *pale faces*.

The legal title of the President to his office in unques-
tioned. There is not only no mode or means by which it
can be brought into question, but there is no ground on
which it could be assailed. In his inauguration, every
theory of constitutional law, no matter how variant, was
fully satisfied. The certificates containing the electoral .
votes were opened by the President of the Senate, in the
presence of both Houses of Congress, the votes were then
counted and the result declared. They were counted and
declared by the presiding officer of the Senate, with the
concurring authority of both Houses, acting under a law,
passed by Congress and approved by the Executive, providing the mode by which the count should be made and the
result ascertained and declared. In case of dispute con-
cerning the electoral vote of a State, from which but one
certificate had been made and forwarded, the vote as certified it was provided, should be counted unless both Houses
concurred in rejecting it. When two or more certificates
were forwarded, the question what votes should be counted
as the votes of that State, were referred to a special tribunal
—the Electoral Commission—created by law for that purpose and empowered to decide every question arising before it, as fully as by law Congress itself could do, whose
decision, it was, by the law of its creation, enacted, should
stand as the decision of the two Houses, unless overruled
by their joint dissent.

This law was passed by a Democratic House and a Republican Senate. It was supported by every Democratic
Senator but one, and by the great body of Democratic
members of the House, with almost the like unanimity.

It was advocated on all sides, as a measure, which would insure not only a peaceful, but a satisfactory settlement of the threatening controversies which had arisen in reference to the result of the Presidential election; and to that end, abundant assurances were publicly given in debate, that whatever might be the decision of the tribunal, it would not only be accepted, but acquiesced in, as conclusive and incapable of being questioned.

And yet what do we now see? An attempt to reopen, for partisan discussion, the whole question of this Presidential Settlement, not only as to its correctness in point of law, but as to its good faith. I know of nothing meaner or more unmanly in our party history. The spirit and determination of this reckless and unscrupulous opposition became manifest in the course of the Presidential Count; and when it had become apparent, from the decisions of the Electoral Commission, that the hopes of a favorable result to the Democratic candidates must be disappointed, an open and combined effort to defeat the proceeding, with whatever consequences to the peace and well-being of the country, was revealed and even proclaimed, in violation of law, on the part of a large number of Democratic members who had voted for the bill, and who favored it, as long as they thought it would secure them a party advantage. How they can reconcile such a course to a nice sense of personal honor, is a problem for themselves to solve, if they consider it of any importance. The country owes much, in the defeat of this revolutionary attempt, to the firmness of Mr. Randall, the Speaker, and to the parliamentary skill and the patriotism of Mr. Fernando Wood, and to the honorable and manly resistance of many Southern Democratic members. Conspicuous upon the side of the disturbers of the public peace were most of the Democratic delegation from this State, particularly those who, at the last popular election for Congressmen, had failed to obtain the indorsement of their constituents, and who, during their Congressional career, having made but little, if any, reputation for useful abilities, seemed determined, at least, to demonstrate that they had a talent for mischief.

It is alleged, in extenuation of their attempted repudia-
tion of their own work, by Democratic politicians, that
the Electoral Commission was a purely partisan body, deciding every question in accordance with the party bias of
a majority of its members. It is, indeed, true that all material decisions of the tribunal were rendered, upon votes,
on which the Democratic members voted one way and the
Republican members another. But the controversy was
political in its nature, and the differences between the parties, it ought not to be denied, were honestly entertained.
Is it any more to be wondered at that Republicans should
believe their own party to be right than that Democrats
should be subject to a similar infatuation? But the com-
plaint is unjust and puerile. It ought to have been made,
if at all, against the very constitution of the Commission
itself, for the very principle of its organization was to divide it equally in membership between the two parties, taking five from the House and five from the Senate, and four
from the bench of the Supreme Court, with a fifth judge,
to be the fifteenth Commissioner, selected by agreement of
the four judges already chosen, and who, of course, had to
belong to one or the other of the two parties. If this
choice had fallen on a Democrat, there is no expectation
that the decisions would have been less partisan than they
were, though there is reason to suppose that the Democrats
would not then have been the complaining party.

But it is said that the Commission refused to hear evidence which they were bound to receive. But the question
of whether it was competent for them, by law, to receive
and hear evidence, was one of the very questions the Tribunal was organized to decide. The title of the act was,
" *To provide for and regulate the counting of votes for President and Vice-President, and the decision of questions arising
thereon,*" etc. It provided, in the case of two conflicting
returns from any State, that they should "*be submitted to
the judgment and decision as to which is the true and lawful
electoral vote of such State,*" of the Commission constituted
thereby. The returns, and papers accompanying them,
and the objections thereto, in all such cases, were required

to be submitted to the Commission, " which shall proceed," says the statute, " to consider the same, with the same powers, if any, now possessed for that purpose by the two houses acting separately or together, and by a majority of votes decide whether any and what votes from such States are the votes provided for by the Constitution of the United States, and how many and what persons were duly appointed Electors in such State, *and may therein take into view such petitions, depositions, and other papers, if any, as shall by the Constitution and now existing laws be competent and pertinent in such consideration.*" The Democratic objectors and counsel offered to submit certain testimony to impeach the validity of the Republican returns from certain States. This was objected to as not competent evidence. The question was argued, and decided by the Commission, sustaining the objections and ruling out the testimony offered.

That the Commission, in reaching this result, were in the rightful exercise of admitted jurisdiction, is sufficiently manifest from the terms of the law. That the particular result reached was in the contemplation of those who advocated the passage of the law, is shown by the debates upon the bill when pending in Congress.

Senator Thurman, in a speech in favor of the bill (January 24, 1877), said :

" All that we could do was to constitute a tribunal as honest and impartial and fair as we could make it, as likely to be intelligent and learned and honest as we could find, and as likely to command the respect of the country as any we could frame, and submit to that, as we submit to our Supreme Judicial Tribunal, the Supreme Court of the United States, the constitutional questions that are involved in this subject."

He then proceeds to enumerate the questions of this character that had already arisen, and specifies eleven, on which parties had divided, and said :

" The decision of any one of these propositions in this bill, if it could be made, would most probably decide the present contest in regard to who is President-elect."

Among them he specifies the question, whether it is
competent to go behind the certificate of the Governor,
whether it is competent to go behind the decision of a canvassing or returning board, to impeach it for want of jurisdiction, or for fraud, etc.; and continuing his argument,
said:

"Sir, we took the only course that was open to us; we
provided a tribunal, just as individuals who can not settle
their controversies, must go to the Courts in order that they
may be settled by a judicial tribunal. Just so, when these
two houses can not agree, they must call in the benefit of an
honest, an able, and a learned tribunal, and weigh its decision before they ultimately decide; and that is all that
this bill does. *Therefore it is that this bill leaves every question to this tribunal, with the power, as I said before, of review
and reversal by the two houses.*"

The very point was distinctly brought out when Senator
Morton, who opposed the bill, offered an amendment, as
follows:

"*Provided*, That nothing herein contained shall author-
ize the said Commission to go behind the finding and determination of the canvassing or returning officers of a
State, authorized by the laws of the State to find and determine the result of an election for electors."

Senator Edmunds, who supported the bill, "in order," as
he said, "to guard against the slant which the rejection of
this amendment might in some minds produce in respect
of the opinions of the passers of this bill," moved to amend
the amendment so that it should read:

"That the said Commission shall have authority to go
behind the finding and determination of the canvassing or
returning officers," etc.

Both propositions were rejected, thus leaving the bill to
stand without an implication either way, and leaving the
question of its own jurisdiction open, for the decision of
the Commission, upon the Constitution and the existing
laws.

The question of the correctness of the decisions of the
Tribunal is one that, considering the character of the men

who composed it, ought not now to be mooted as a political issue : yet the principles of constitutional law affirmed by them are of permanent interest. They are few and simple, and need only to be clearly stated to be understood and vindicated.

They may be stated as follows :

1. The choice of Presidential Electors, to be made by each State in the manner provided by its Legislature, is a matter solely within the jurisdiction of the State.

2. That when the choice has been made, the form and expression and record of it constituting the fact of a complete process, with an ascertained and declared result, is irrevocable and unimpeachable ; unless in some mode and by some authority provided by the State itself, as a part of the verification of the proceeding.

3. That any such correction of an apparent choice must be had, if at all, before the time when the designated electors are required by federal law, to perform the function of their office, by actually casting the vote of the State. When that time has arrived, the whole matter passes the line that divides, on this subject, the State and Federal jurisdictions.

4. That the canvass and record of the election constitutes the fact of the election, and is the official and unimpeachable declaration of its result : but the certificate of that fact, given by a certifying officer, is but an instrument of evidence, which, if false, may be corrected by a comparison with the recorded fact, to which it professes to correspond.

Applying these principles to the controverted cases, the Commission decided, that the persons declared to have been chosen electors in Florida, Louisiana, and South Carolina by the boards or officers, who were charged with that duty by law, were the true electors for that State ; that the proceedings in Florida, subsequent to the casting of the electoral vote, by which it was sought to set aside the prior action of the State, were null, and without jurisdiction ; and that, in counting the electoral votes, it was not competent for Congress to enter into a contest over the title of any of the electors ; but that in the case of Oregon, where

the Governor falsely certified the election of an elector,
when by the canvass and record of the election itself, another appeared and had been declared to have been elected,
Congress had the right and was bound to receive the fact
and reject the false certificate.

Candid men of all parties must ultimately acknowledge
the soundness of these principles. The distinguished Senator from Delaware (Mr. Bayard) in a speech in the Senate
on February 25, 1875, substantially affirmed them. He
said :

"And nowhere is power given to either House of Congress to pass upon the election, either the manner or the
fact, of electors for the President and Vice-President ; and
if the Congress of the United States, either one or both
Houses, shall assume, under the guise or pretext of telling
or counting a vote to decide the fact of the election of electors who are to form the college by whom the President
and Vice-President are to be chosen, then they will have
taken upon themselves an authority for which I, for one,
can find no warrant in this charter of limited powers."
. . . "There is no pretext that for any cause whatever Congress has any power, or all the other departments
of the Government have any power to refuse to receive
and count the result of the action of the voters in the States
in that election as certified by the electors whom they have
chosen. That questions may arise whether that choice was
made, that questions may arise whether that election was
properly held or whether it was a free and fair election, is
undoubtedly true; but there is no machinery provided for
contest, and no contest seems to have been anticipated on
this subject. It is *casus omissus*, intentionally or otherwise,
upon the part of those who framed this government, and
we must take it as it is, and if there be necessity for its
amendment, for its supplement, that must be the action of
the American people in accordance with the constitution
itself; and I am free to say that some amendment on this
subject should be had."

The legal validity of the President's title to his office, invested with every required formal security, and based on

the soundest, and fundamental constitutional principles, must, I think, be unanimously affirmed. But it may still be said that it is without the essential support of a moral right.

It would seem rather a difficult undertaking, in a matter, involving no private interest, but simply a question of public right, to attack successfully a valid legal title to a public office, acquiesced in by the people, who alone have any rights to it, on the alleged ground of a moral defect. Certainly, no incumbent, with a perfect legal title, can be called a *usurper* of an office; and, with equal certainty, it ought to be admitted that nothing short of personal participation in fraudulent practices clearly proven, which have been used successfully as an instrument of intrusion, should subject any man to the odious charge. No greater outrage upon the elective franchise was ever attempted than that which was involved in the effort to count the vote of Cronin, as an Elector of Oregon. Yet, if, on grounds of technical law, it had prevailed—or what, under the circumstances, was equivalent, the vote of Watts had been rejected, as every Democratic member of the Commission voted to do—would Mr. Tilden, on that account, have declined Inauguration—would Mr. Chas. Francis Adams have scornfully refused to become his Secretary of State? Such suppositions are not within the limits of the probable.

The responsibility of political parties to the people for their conduct, and the conduct of their leaders and organs, in reference to the freedom and purity of elections, can not and ought not to be denied. They must be held to strict account for the observance of the rules of morality, and for sincere respect for popular rights in all their political conduct. No party has, perhaps, been altogether free from offenses of this description; and yet the Republican party, I think, has a right to claim a contrast between itself and the Democratic party, in that particular, not favorable to its adversary. The frauds in Plaquemine Parish, in Louisiana, in 1844, were never censured by those in whose interest they were perpetrated; while corruption of the ballot, as of every other political agency, incorporated in the

Tammany Society of the city of New York, the headquarters of Democratic party politics, has delivered that great city and State into the power of a series of "bosses," who dictate legislation and divide offices with impartial effrontery. In our own State, we have had recent illustration of its evil power. Two Congressional Districts are believed to have been carried for Democratic candidates by *repeaters*, hired and paid out of the party treasury, some of whom are even now paying the penalty of their crimes in our jails and penitentiaries. But the most convincing proof of the contrast is that the Republican party has systematically sought to guard and protect the ballot, so as to secure free and fair elections; and to that end, in our last General Assembly, passed a Registry Law, of the least onerous and stringent character, whose simple and most unobjectionable features are reproached by the Democratic State Convention as discriminating against the poor!

It is said, however, that the Republican party, as a National party, is responsible for the frauds charged against the Returning Board of Louisiana ; if not by reason of previous instigation, then by subsequent ratification and adoption.

Of the personal integrity of the members of that Board, the purity of their motives, the uprightness of their intentions, no one is called to be sponsor, because no one is competent to judge. I have, speaking for myself, seen no evidence whatever that justifies the cruel and unmerciful abuse to which they have been subject. Their imprisonment by the last House of Representatives, as public officers of a State, for merely refusing to surrender public archives belonging to the State, no longer in their possession, and which, if in their custody, they ought not to surrender, was, to my mind, not merely a vindictive persecution, but was among the grossest violations of personal right, and the grossest indignities to State authority ever perpetrated under sanction of a Federal power—a precedent full of danger to both private and public right. That they were not personally corrupt in the exercise of their official functions, in the canvass of the election in November, was sufficiently established in my convictions by the fact that they were not corrupted! If they had been what they are now charged with being, the probability is that Democratic *charity* would have been larger than the Democratic *conscience*, and would have covered and concealed their sin as with a garment—even the garment of praise!

But what we have to do with is the *acts*, not the *motives*, of these men. What did they which constitutes their offense?

The statements of the votes cast in the various parishes and voting precincts, which came into their hands officially, and from which they were required to make up their return of the election, showed, if compiled without correction, an apparent majority of some thousands for the Tilden electors.

It also, however, appeared that this apparent majority was mainly composed of heavy Democratic majorities in five parishes, in which, at the last election held, a year before, the majorities had been more largely the other way, and that there had been in operation no causes likely to produce in them any marked change of political opinion. In one of these parishes it appeared that not a single Republican vote had been cast.

It further appeared that in these five parishes particularly, and elsewhere throughout the State, beginning with the opening of the political campaign in the spring of the year, and continuing until the very day of the election, an illegal military organization had patrolled the State, with the avowed purpose, by displays of violence and the infliction of violence, of preventing the colored voters of the State from voting for the Republican candidates. This fact, in my opinion, is fully proven. I do not believe that its substantial truth will be denied by intelligent and candid persons, of any party, acquainted with the facts. I do not stop now to consider the provocations and excuses alleged in its palliation. The fact is that alone which is now material. Its effect was palpable and notorious. It had been efficient, to a large extent, in destroying the legitimate Republican vote, and thus had prevented a fair and free election.

The duty in these circumstances of the Returning Officers

was prescribed by the Constitution and laws of Louisiana.

The 103d Article of the Constitution declared that "the privilege of free suffrage shall be supported by laws regulating elections, and prohibiting, under adequate penalties, all undue influence thereon from power, bribery, tumult, or other improper practice."

The Election Laws of the State expressly made it the duty of the Returning Officers, in case they should be convinced of the existence of any of the enumerated causes, which materially interfered with the purity and freedom of the election at any voting place, to exclude from their returns the statements of the poll at such place.

This, and this only, is what this Board did in canvassing and compiling the votes at the Presidential election, purging the election of results effected by intimidation and violence, so as to restore, as nearly as could be done, the purity, fairness and freedom of the election. As it was, it was but an approximation; for they could not restore to the ballot-box the thousands of votes, which, through fear, the voters had failed to deposit. And it can not reasonably be doubted that if the election had been allowed to take place peaceably and without intimidation and violence, the majority of votes actually cast would have been largely in favor of the Republican candidates.

An outcry has been made against this alleged disfranchisement of voters, who may not themselves have been guilty of the forfeiting cause; but no principle in the law of elections is better settled, or settled upon better reasons than this: that an election, which is not fair and free, is no election at all. If the vote, as actually cast, is the final test of the election, without regard to how, and by whom, and under what circumstances cast, and regardless, too, of those which have, by unfair means, been prevented from being cast, then an election, instead of being a peaceful comparison of opinions, will be simply a struggle of physical strength, deciding which party has superior force.

In strange contrast to these Democratic complaints in reference to the correction of the election returns from

Louisiana by the officers charged by law with that duty, so as to purge the election from the vicious effects of violence and intimidation, are the positions taken by the Democratic objectors and counsel in the case of South Carolina before the Electoral Commission. In that case the objections made to the Republican Electoral vote were, in substance:

1. That the election was void, because the Legislature of the State had failed to execute a provision of the State Constitution requiring the passage of Registry Laws.

2. That the election was void by reason of intimidation, caused partly by the mere presence of troops of the United States, sent there by the President on the call of the Governor, to preserve the peace; and by intimidation alleged to have been practiced by both whites and blacks, Democrats and Republicans. Mr. Hurd, of Ohio, who represented the Democratic objectors in this case, admitted the principle, that "if lawlessness prevail so that it is impossible there should be a lawful election; if violence is practiced, so that men are not able freely to go to the polls; if intimidation be practiced, so that large numbers of men who would otherwise vote, do not go near the polls, or who, if they do go to the polls, are compelled to vote against their will, then an election, held under such circumstances, is held in a condition of anarchy, in which a republic is a mere myth and a fiction."

In order, therefore, to invalidate the election in South Carolina, and to reject its electoral vote entirely from the Count, he claimed the right to prove, not merely the intimidation by Republicans of Democratic voters, but in addition said:

"We propose to show by the testimony which was taken by the minority of the Committee that in counties which gave large Democratic majorities the Democratic leaders and managers interfered with the freedom of the election by practicing intimidation upon their black employes and those who might happen to live within their district. We propose to show that rifle clubs were organized, which were not disbanded in accordance with the proclamation of the

President of the United States, *and that under the effects of these rifle clubs, and the intimidation that was practiced in that method, large numbers of negroes, who otherwise would have voted the Republican ticket, voted the Democratic ticket."*

In conclusion, therefore, I think we may venture to claim, with the greatest confidence, that there is no occasion that the Democratic party in this State should, as its Convention declares it does, " look upon the inauguration of R. B. Hayes to the high office of President of the United States " " as the most dangerous encroachment upon popular rights that has ever been attempted in this or any other free country ;" that it was not accomplished " in spite of a majority of the electoral vote and popular vote given by the people to Samuel J. Tilden," but that, on the contrary, it was the peaceful triumph of constitutional principles, vindicating the freedom of the elective franchise against a wide-spread and dangerous conspiracy, which sought by force and fear to suppress the expression of the popular will, and threatened, in the rage of party disappointment, in violation of plighted faith, and in defiance of law, to plunge the country into all the perils of anarchy and civil war.

The discussion of this question is not wholly without practical interest. The peaceful inauguration of President Hayes was a narrow escape from a great danger, and its practical lesson to us is to provide, by necessary constitutional amendments, against the recurrence of such a peril. The unsatisfactory mode now provided for the election of the President and Vice-President of the United States is fully demonstrated. It does not at all fulfill the intention which created it, and has developed difficulties and dangers against which it provides no remedy or security.

The plan of an amendment substantially like that proposed and advocated by Senator Morton ought, without further delay, to be perfected, proposed, and adopted. That plan abolishes the Electoral College as unnecessary ; while it preserves the Electoral votes of the several States, according to the original law of representative proportion, but divides the vote of each State, so as to secure a safe and more perfect popular representation. This will diminish fraud, by lessening the temptation to fraud, and with means provided for contested Electoral returns, will, as nearly as can be, constitute a safeguard for the peaceful exercise, by free and fair elections, of the elective franchise. It will prevent the concentrated votes of large civic communities like that of such cities as New York, from carrying with it the adverse majority of the remainder of the State, and thus unduly suppressing the legitimate influence of large minorities. It will bring the election nearer to the people without in any wise weakening the relative influence and power of the States; and will tend most powerfully to break up party divisions based on class or sectional lines. Coupled with a provision limiting the tenure of the Presidential office to a single term, we shall express in the terms of the Constitution, as Presidential qualifications, that disinterestedness, modesty, and wholehearted zeal for the public good, which, as natural qualities, adorn and grace the present incumbent; and thus we shall vindicate the integrity of his election, by incorporating his example into the fundamental law.

THE SOUTHERN POLICY.

The inauguration of President Hayes, preceded and surrounded by circumstances so anomalous and unprecedented, brought him almost immediately face to face with the delicate and difficult duty of dealing with what has been called the Southern question.

The situation was this. Concurrently with the Presidential election, State elections had taken place in South Carolina and Louisiana, at which two sets of claimants for possession of the offices of the State asserted their exclusive right, each claiming to be lawfully entitled. Chamberlain and Hampton represented the rival claims in South Carolina; Packard and Nicholls were the contestants in Louisiana. Each attempted, as against the other, the exclusive exercise of the administration of the State government. The facts of both cases being substantially alike, and the same principles applicable equally to both, it will be more satisfactory and convenient to consider by itself the case as it was presented in Louisiana.

Troops of the United States in New Orleans, under prior orders, were instructed to prevent the threatened conflict. The Packard government occupied the State-house and had possession of the records and archives of certain offices; but its authority was recognized only in small areas in the State, outside of New Orleans, and in that city scarcely at all outside of the State-house. Each set of claimants had installed themselves in part, neither in whole. The legislative body itself divided. Part adhered to one government and part to another. Nicholls had a quorum of the Senate, having certificates of election from the Returning Board, with those holding over; while a quorum of the House of Representatives, holding similar certificates, adhered to Packard. There was, in fact, no single organization that constituted the government of Louisiana, as contemplated by its constitution and laws.

President Grant had instructed the officer in command of the Federal troops to use them so as to preserve the actual status as between the hostile parties, and prevent collision. He subsequently modified the order so as to limit the duty of the military force to the preservation of the peace, leaving each government to exercise such functions as it could exert or acquire without a breach of the peace. He had declined from the beginning to recognize either as the rightful government of the State, or to employ force to establish and maintain its claims.

When President Hayes came into office, he continued in force the same orders. In due time, he organized a Commission of gentlemen, of high character, to proceed to New Orleans in order personally to view the situation, and to report, not upon the abstract and technical title of either government, but whether such a condition of things existed, as required the presence and intervention of the military force of the United States, and what would probably result from a withdrawal of the troops. It is perhaps true, and may be considered as having been made publicly known, that it was his intention to withdraw the troops, as soon as it could be done, without danger to life and property and the public peace. Before the Commission had completed their observations, and, no doubt, under the influence of the belief that the United States would not enforce by arms the claims of the Packard government, the members of the Legislature, until that time adhering to that government, went over to the Nicholls' Legislature, and were admitted to seats as members of it. And then, that Legislature, in both branches, had a quorum of members, holding certificates of election from the Returning Board. The Packard government dissolved, and the troops were sent to their barracks. This is an outline of that course of events, which, so far as they were brought about by the action or failure to act of the Administration, has been called its Southern Policy.

It may be assumed, for the purposes of this inquiry, that the Packard was, as it claimed to be, the legitimate and lawfully elected government, Packard himself having been declared to have been elected by a legislature, which at the time, had, in each branch, a quorum of members, having *prima facie* title to seats, by virtue of certificates of election from the Returning Board, including Senators who held over.

But it must also be assumed that the Packard government had no hold upon its constituency—that the wealth, property, and physical and moral force of the community were arrayed against it and determined not to submit to its establishment—that in point of fact, it was not able to exercise any of the functions of government in any effective and substantial manner or to any useful extent—that nothing but the presence of the military power of the United States, acting under the orders, already referred to, secured to it, the semblance of even a formal existence—that, without that, it could not have organized, and in the event of its withdrawal would have been hopelessly dispersed, without the ability to make even a show of resistance. In other words, that while the Packard government was the *de jure* or titular government, the Nicholls government was the government *de facto*.

I know it is claimed on behalf of the Packard government that if it had received the moral support of recognition by the Federal Executive and its military aid, it could have overthrown the Nicholls government; and that, when that had been accomplished the troops of the United States could have been withdrawn, without danger to the peace of the State. This no doubt was the opinion of Mr. Packard himself. If, however, the determination of the fact, in question, is material to the issue, the President of the United States had the right to form an opinion upon it for himself, indeed was bound so to do, for he is invested by the Constitution and laws with a discretion, in such cases, to be exercised upon his own judgment of the existence of the facts, in view of which he is to act.

On the other hand, the reasons for the contrary opinion were of the gravest character, and preponderating, if not conclusive. The government represented by Mr. Packard, and that of which his was the successor, without reflecting upon his personal character, was odious to the great body of the native white people of the State. They believed it to be oppressive and corrupt. To it, and its mal-administration, they attributed all the evils of their condition. They believed it to be a usurpation. The Kellogg government never, in their opinion, had been fairly elected. It owed its establishment, according to their view, to fraud and force; and it had been submitted to, for the time, only in the hope of an early deliverance. The establishment of its successor, maintained in the same spirit, they regarded as their ruin. The idea of longer submission had become intolerable. They determined to resist it, by every means, to the last; and although, they would not oppose arms to the military power of the United States, it was, I believe, their determination, to use such means, as would, they thought, secure to them, what they considered, a preferable alternative, a military government by the army of the United States.

It was the existence and strength of this sentiment that gave such power to the Democratic representatives who obstructed the progress, with a view to the defeat of the

Presidential count. They put the case to their colleagues from the Southern States with great force and art. They said, you have nothing to expect from Republican successes, except a perpetuation of the wrongs and abuses of which you complain. Those you intend hereafter to resist, at all hazards, and to every extremity. If the Republican National Administration is prolonged, your struggle will be hopeless, because it will be local, without allies, and illegal; but join us in defeating the Presidential count. The area of the conflict then will be extended to the whole nation, and you will have the aid of the National Democratic party, fighting for its own success as well as yours, and thus you will enlist strength, which, if not sufficient to inaugurate Tilden, upon an election by the House of Representatives, will, at least, insure a new Presidential election, in which every conservative influence will combine in your favor.

To this was opposed the argument of honor and good faith, implied in the passage of the Electoral Commission bill, as a compromise and an arbitration; the evidence, from President Grant's course and declarations, that the army of the United States should not be used to decide questions of the State elections, and the title of conflicting State officers, and assurances that the Republican National Platform, as interpreted by General Hayes' letter of acceptance, was a pledge, given in good faith, that would be sacredly performed, that no State government should be forced upon an unwilling people by Federal bayonets. And without this evidence and these assurances, it is my conviction that the peace of the Nation would have been seriously threatened, if not broken, in an attempt to prevent the orderly and peaceful process of declaring the election and completing the inauguration of the Republican President, and the country convulsed with an interregnum of doubtful constitutionality, and the fierce excitement of a new election, in which party passion would have been inflamed as it never had been before.

But the principal, if not the only material question, recurs. It is simply this: Was the course and conduct of the President justified by the Constitution and the laws?

The fourth section of the fourth article of the Constitution of the United States provides as follows:

"The United States shall guarantee to every State in this Union a republican form of government, and shall protect each of them against invasion, and on application of the Legislature, or of the Executive (when the Legislature can not be convened), against domestic violence."

For the purpose of carrying into effect this constitutional provision, Congress, by the act of February 28, 1795, provided that, "In case of an insurrection in any State against the government thereof, it shall be lawful for the President of the United States, or of the Executive, when the Legislature can not be convened, to call forth such number of the militia of any other State or States as may be applied for, as he may judge sufficient to suppress an insurrection."

By subsequent legislation, the President was authorized, on the same conditions, to use, in lieu of the militia of any of the States, such part of the land or naval forces of the United States as he might deem expedient.

In commenting upon and interpreting these provisions of the Constitution and law, the Supreme Court of the United States, in the well-known case of Luther v. Borden (7 Howard's Reports, 43), which grew out of the Dorr rebellion in Rhode Island, laid down the doctrine of the following extract:

"By this act, the power of deciding whether the exigency had arisen upon which the government of the United States is bound to interfere, is given to the President. He is to act upon the application of the Legislature, or of the Executive, and, consequently, he must determine what body of men constitute the Legislature, and who is the Governor, before he can act. The fact that both parties claim the right to the government can not alter the case, for both can not be entitled to it. If there is an armed conflict, like the one of which we are speaking, it is a case of domestic violence, and one of the parties must be in insurrection against the lawful government; and the

President must of necessity decide which is the government and which party is unlawfully arrayed against it, before he can perform the duty imposed upon him by the act of Congress."

It will be observed that the discretion conceded here to the President is very wide and far-reaching. It is subordinate only to the authority of Congress, for it is said by the Supreme Court, in this same case:

" Under this article of the Constitution it rests with Congress to decide what government is the established one in a State. For as the United States guarantee to each State a republican form of government, Congress must necessarily decide what government is established in the State before it can determine whether it is republican or not. And when the senators and representatives of a State are admitted into the councils of the Union, the authority of the government under which they are appointed, as well as its republican character, is recognized by the proper constitutional authority. And its decision is binding on every other department of the government, and can not be questioned in a judicial tribunal."

In the absence of any such previous decision by Congress, the President is compelled to exercise his own discretion under the law. That discretion, when exercised, can not be revised, reversed, or reviewed by any other body or tribunal. He is responsible for it, as he is for all other of his political conduct, to the two Houses of Congress, by the process of impeachment, and not otherwise.

It must not be supposed, however, that this discretionary authority of the President is purely personal, arbitrary, and capricious, and subject to no rules for its guidance. Far from that. It is a legal and official discretion, exercised under the most solemn responsibilities, and to be exercised with careful scrutiny of the circumstances which invoke it, with an anxious desire to promote only the public good, and in the spirit of loyalty to the sound principles of free government.

The principles and rules which ought to govern a wise and patriotic executive in the discharge of the delicate responsibilities of such a discretion are obvious, but not on that account unimportant, though more likely to be overlooked.

1. In the first place, this discretion must be exercised only within the limits and upon the conditions prescribed in express terms or by necessary implications in the Constitution and the law. Whatever reasons, and however urgent, may be assigned for intervention, they must find their warrant in the written law. It can lawfully occur, only in the very manner and the very case described. And it is a matter, not without much significance, that the language of the Constitution is much broader than that of the Act of Congress, to execute it. The 4th section of the 4th article of the Constitution says that Congress shall, on the application of the legislature, or of the executive, when the legislature can not be convened, protect each State *against domestic violence*. This constitutional command is laid upon Congress, not upon the President. However imperative upon Congress, it nevertheless leaves with Congress legislative discretion as to what shall constitute the domestic violence against which it is bound by law to protect each State, and in what cases, and in what manner, that protection shall be afforded. The President has no such discretion. He is bound by the Act of Congress, which, in this respect, for him, has conclusively defined the terms of the Constitution.

Congress may not have exhausted all its legislative authority in the laws it has passed. There may be cases of domestic violence in a State, against which protection ought, within the purview of the Constitution, to be furnished. But that duty rests upon Congress, and upon Congress alone. The President is strictly limited by the law, as actually in force, and can not act in cases not contemplated by it, although within the language of the Constitution. And the law limits the action of the President to a single case of domestic violence. Unless it amounts to a case of an *insurrection*, no matter how distinctly otherwise it may be a case of *domestic violence*, the President has no authority of law for his intervention. It is only in the one instance of " *an insurrection in any State against the government thereof,"* that the law confers upon him power to act for the purpose of protecting the State against domestic violence, by suppressing such insurrection.

2. In the second place, the legal discretion vested in the President by the Act of Congress is a discretion *to act* upon the contingency and the conditions prescribed, if he sees fit ; but also, *not to act at all,* if he so determine. The language of the law is, *" it shall be lawful for the President,"* etc. It is not, *" it shall be the duty of the President,"* etc. It does not impose a mere ministerial and positive obligation. He is not only made the judge of who is the Governor, and what body of men constitute the Legislature, and of the sufficiency of the number of troops required, and whether the fact of an insurrection exists ; but also whether, taking all the circumstances into consideration, it is wise and expedient, and for the public good, for him to respond to the requisition. He may not think military intervention necessary. He may think the government of the State sufficiently strong to protect itself. He may think the insurrection temporary and ephemeral, that will, of itself, languish and die out. On the other hand, he may think intervention unavailing. The insurrection may already have gone so far as to have become an accomplished fact. It may have become successful revolution. It may have completely overthrown the old and previously established government, and firmly planted another in its stead. The alleged insurrection may, in fact, be nothing but a violent and unavailing effort of the old order to restore its power and authority by displacing that which, although new and revolutionary, has nevertheless become fixed and accepted. He may, therefore, conclude that the insurrection, if such it can be called, ought not to be suppressed ; but that, having succeeded, for the sake of the public peace and tranquillity, it ought not to be disturbed by force. The whole question, therefore, whether there shall be any intervention at all, supposing every contingency of the law to have happened, and every condition fulfilled, is a question of policy and public expediency, remitted for decision

to the sound discretion of the President, to be exercised by
him with sole reference to the probable good or ill consequences of acting or refusing to act.

3. In the third place, the President ought not to exercise his discretion affirmatively in favor of an intervention
in a doubtful case. The employment of the military force
ought not to be an ordinary function of civil government
in its internal administration. There is an American prejudice against standing armies, which ought not to be dis-
couraged—*Inter leges, arma silent.* Force, it is true, lies
couched behind all law; but it is best that it should remain
hid, and not displayed. Resort to armed power should be
a refuge only in time of imminent and extreme danger,
and should never be permitted to supersede, except in cases
of absolute necessity, the peaceful methods of legal process, or the still more wholesome and efficacious restraints
of a resolute public opinion. Any government, whatever
its form, which depends habitually, in the course of its ordinary administration, upon its military power, has already
ceased to be free; and a people, however brave and high-
spirited, that are obliged to live in the shadow of its con-
stant menace, will become unfit for and incapable of the
duties and responsibilities of citizenship. The republican
institutions, of which we are justly proud, can be maintained only by the voluntary and intelligent co-operation
of a free and united people, who feel and act as though,
notwithstanding the diversity of individual character and
interests, they are bound together as one homogeneous and
indivisible commonwealth, instinct with the consciousness
of a common national life and destiny. I would not un-
derestimate the spirit and service of our gallant little army.
It protects, with many sacrifices, our frontier settlements
against the warfare of the savage, and is the nucleus which,
in time of public peril, gathers and organizes and inspires
the martial spirit of the people. But the army is for war;
in time of peace, let us look only to the coercion of the law
and the moral support of a vigorous public opinion to hold
in subjection all the elements of disorder. This country
can not be governed by bayonets; it can be governed only

by ideas. Let us not, even in the presence of new and un-
expected and dangerous assaults upon the order and institutions of society, be carried away from our safe and accustomed moorings, lest we drift into dangerous currents and
upon fatal rocks. Let us beware, lest expedients, introduced as experiments and exceptions, are drawn into prece-
dents against the regular course of constitutional life ; lest,
in place of a tonic, we inject a poison into the veins and
arteries of the body politic.

In reference to the application of this rule, in regulating
the discretion of the President, in the use of troops to sup-
press insurrection in a State, the language of Mr. Caleb
Cushing, when Attorney-General, in his opinion to the
President, in the case of the Vigilance Committee of San
Francisco, is strong but just. He says :

" This, however, it seems safe to say, that the application
of this high power of the President to cases of doubtful
legal condition ought to be reserved for circumstances of
the most exigent emergency ; such as, for instance, a case
of indisputable *bellum flagrans* in a given State, and in
which all the constitutional power of the State shall have
been exerted in vain to prevent or suppress domestic war,
and in which also imminent or extreme public disaster can
be arrested only by such interposition of the Federal government." (8 Attorney-General's Op. 14.)

4. But probably the most important rule for the regulation of this discretion of the President is deduced from its
very nature, as being *political* and not *judicial*. If it were
judicial in its nature, then it would necessarily follow that
the question for decision would have to be examined and
tried according to the course of judicial procedure ; by the
examination of witnesses, the production of proofs, trial
by jury, and review by judicial tribunals. In the language
of the Supreme Court in the case already quoted (*Luther*
v. *Borden*), " If the judicial power extends so far, the guarantee contained in the Constitution of the United States is
a guarantee of anarchy and not of order."

The discretion vested in the President, then, is a political
power, not to be exercised judicially, for the purpose of

trying and establishing legal rights, but proceeding only on grounds of policy and wise expediency. In deciding the question, so far as it is necessary for him to decide it, in the exercise of his discretion to use military force in the suppression of insurrection, it is no part of his duty to inquire into the title of either contesting government. The point of investigation and interest is, not where is the *right*, having reference to the regularity and legality of its title, but what is the *fact*—which is the actual and established government, in possession of power, whose authority is recognized by the community, and which is able to maintain its existence firmly and administer the functions of government effectually. The Supreme Court of the United States has affirmed this principle. In the case already quoted (*Luther* v. *Borden*), it says :

"In the case of foreign nations, the government acknowledged by the President is always recognized in the courts of justice. And this principle has been applied by the act of Congress to the sovereign States of the Union." And Mr. Justice Woodbury, in his dissenting opinion in that case, said : "The doctrines laid down in Palmer's case are as directly applicable to this, in the event of two contending parties in arms in a domestic war, as in a foreign. If one is recognized by the Executive or Legislature of the Union as the *de facto* government, the judiciary can only conform to that political decision. . . . The same rule has been applied by this Court in case of a contest as to which is the true constitution between two, or which possesses the true legislative power in, one of our own States—those citizens acting under the new, which is objected to as irregularly made, or those under the old territorial government therein."

It is further to be remarked that the principal question for the Presidential decision is simply whether, under all the circumstances, he shall employ the military forces of the United States as requested. The question which of two rivals is the lawful government is merely incidental to that, and only to be decided as necessary to the determination of the other. It is only as and when he determines to in-

tervene with the military arm that he decides any question
as to the claims of the parties. If he decides not to intervene, he decides nothing else. Above all, the question,
which is the rightful government, can never be submitted
to him separately for decision. That would be to make
him arbiter or judge, and the constitution has not, in such
case, made him a divider of the inheritance between liti-
gants.

Guided by these principles in the exercise of his lawful
discretion, influenced by considerations of what seemed
to him the wisest public policy, President Hayes, after a
careful survey of the actual condition of public affairs in
Louisiana, resolved not to use the army of the United
States to overthrow the Nicholls government, and to establish and maintain the Packard government.

It is this policy that is indorsed by the Republican party
of Ohio, when, in their recent State Convention at Cleveland, they—

"*Resolved*, That the Republicans of Ohio reaffirm their
unfaltering confidence in Rutherford B. Hayes as a statesman, patriot, and Republican, and cordially approve and
support his efforts for the pacification of the country," etc.

It has commanded the congratulations and extorted the
praise of our political opponents, although it has taken
away the largest part of their party capital. It has been
received and accepted with general satisfaction and a sense
of relief from embittered political and sectional agitations
by the people generally. It has given peace and tranquillity
and revived hope to the South. The great body of the
people in South Carolina and Louisiana, of all parties, conditions, and races, have not only acquiesced in it, but recognize it as the dawn of an era of peace, good will, public
and private prosperity, and good government. It has removed prejudices, conciliated those who were alienated,
tended to heal the breaches of the civil war, aroused and
revived a growing and healthy sentiment of nationality,
where before it was weak. It has imposed upon the gov-
erning forces of public opinion and administration in the
reconstructed States a new and deeper sense of political re-

sponsibility, and brought them under voluntary vows to respect and enforce the guarantees of the amended Constitution in support of the equal rights and franchises of the emancipated and colored race. So far, at least, it has wrought good, and not evil. If the people of South Carolina and Louisiana—those who have heretofore voted with the Republican party, and expect to do so hereafter included—more interested in this settlement than any and all others, are satisfied, who has a right to complain?

Nevertheless, there are others who complain and criticise; and as they are of that household of political faith whose principles of public policy the President was chosen to carry into the administration of the National Government, their complaints and criticisms are entitled to respectful consideration, and such answer as can justly be made.

It is objected that the President, in adopting the course pursued, failed in his constitutional and legal duty. This is, indeed, a serious charge. If made good, it leaves him without defense, but if repelled, it would seem that nothing else could be alleged; for if it can be shown that he performed his whole legal duty, certainly nothing more can be required.

The objection assumes that the Packard government was the government of Louisiana, entitled to be recognized as such; that the Nicholls government and its supporters constituted an insurrection against it; that on the requisition of the former he was imperatively bound to employ the army of the United States in its support by suppressing and dispersing the latter, or that if he had any lawful discretion, considerations of wise public policy demanded that he should so act.

The existence and character of such discretion, together with the rules for its just guidance, have already been pointed out; and their statement goes far to furnish the refutation of the objections made.

But there are numerous additional considerations that strengthen and confirm their effect.

In the first place, instead of being a conclusive circumstance in determining the question that Packard was duly and rightfully elected, as has been admitted, it is entirely foreign to the inquiry, and, as the case stood, immaterial. The fact to be ascertained was, what was the government of Louisiana—there were two claimants—not which was the government that had been lawfully chosen, but which was the actual government of the State? The title of Packard may have been perfect; but it was a mere paper title. The possession of Nicholls was complete. With what show of reason can a government, formal in its organization, complete in its possession, asserting its authority under color of right, and claiming title, exercising all the functions of regular administration according to the course of peaceful procedure, passing laws, administering justice, levying and collecting taxes, firmly established and cheerfully obeyed by the people, almost unanimously—how, I say, can such a government be called an insurrection? And, on the other hand, how can that be called the actual and lawful government of a State, which consists of a Governor, and State officers, and a legislative body, shut up within the walls of a single building, protected there from capture by the troops of the Federal Government, and capable of exercising none of the authority of law, or commanding the obedience of a constituency? As well might Henri of Bourbon, or the Count of Paris, or the Prince Imperial, claim that Marshal McMahon and the French people were in a state of insurrection against their several legitimate and rightful governments!

The fact is too palpable to be further dwelt upon, that there was no case under the law of an insurrection against the government the State. Of this, the demonstration was complete when the adherents of the Packard government realized the President's determination not to use military force to assert their title. The whole appearance of any such government immediately dissolved into thin air and nothingness.

It may be replied that this view is based on the maxim that "might makes right," ignores the rights of majorities, and is fatal to the idea of republican government. But this is not at all to the point. The question relates to the duty of the President under a statute, precise and definite in its terms; and the argument must not wander from the case. Under this statute, the President is not charged with the duty of guaranteeing the republican character of the government of a State. That is a separate duty, and belongs to Congress alone.

The same objection is turned into an *argumentum ad hominem*, and with a popular and plausible turn it is alleged that, as Packard received a larger majority, even of the popular vote, than was given to the Republican electors, the President was estopped to deny the validity of Packard's claim, and by refusing to recognize and maintain it, has impeached his own title as President. But the fallacy of this pretension has been already exposed. The argument in defense of the President's course and decision proceeds on the assumption that Packard received a majority of votes and was duly elected, by showing that notwithstanding that, the statutory case, in which alone the President could intervene, did not exist. The question of Packard's election was never before the President for decision; and, in point of fact, he never passed upon it.

But the President is arraigned for having a policy on this subject at all, that could be called presidential; and a policy, appropriately so described, is stigmatized as an anomaly and offense—as savoring of bad faith—as having a native and historical odor of treachery and intrigue. And it is distinctly charged as being in violation of the pledges given to the National Republican party, by the acceptance of its nomination and its platform, on the faith of which the President received its political support. The specification under this head is, that he has violated that section of the Republican platform which reads as follows:

"The permanent pacification of the Southern section of the Union and the complete protection of all its citizens in the free enjoyment of all their rights, are duties to which the Republican party stands sacredly pledged. The power to provide for the enforcement of the principles embodied in the recent constitutional amendments is vested by those amendments in the Congress of the United States, and we declare it to be the solemn obligation of the Government to put into immediate and vigorous exercise all its constitutional powers for removing any just causes of discontent on the part of any class, and for securing to every American citizen complete liberty and exact equality in the exercise of all civil, political, and public rights. To this end, we imperatively demand a Congress and a Chief Executive whose courage and fidelity shall not falter until the results are placed beyond dispute or recall."

It is altogether unreasonable to denounce the President for having a policy of his own, when the matter in hand is a question of the proper exercise of legal discretion vested in the Executive alone. He is compelled to act, in his official character, under the sanction and responsibility of his oath of office, and with the aid of his constitutional advisers, adopt the course that seems to him right and wise. Whatever policy he pursues becomes, by the fact of his pursuing it, the Presidential policy. It is hardly worth while to quarrel with a name.

But as to the substance of the charge, I venture to say that it will puzzle the ingenuity of the most astute faultfinder, to point out wherein the measures of the President, now in question, violate the pledges of the Republican platform. Certainly he has not failed in his efforts to secure " the permanent pacification of the Southern section of the Union," nor in putting forth his " constitutional powers for removing just causes of discontent on the part of any class;" and as to " the complete protection of all its citizens in the free enjoyment of all their rights," and the enforcement of the principles of the constitutional amendments, in what has he omitted any thing he ought or could have done? If he has not kept these Republican pledges, it is because he has acted in contravention of the amendments of the Constitution ; and it would be more to the purpose to charge him with a violation of his duty to the Constitution than of the promises of his party. But what have these amendments to do with the question of recognizing and sustaining the Packard government by military force in Louisiana? The accusation needs only to be put in form to reduce it to absurdity. If the maintenance by force of Republican party governments in the reconstructed States is a necessary means to the enforcement of the rights guaranteed by the amendments to the Constitution, then the duty to uphold them is an imperative and constitutional necessity, absolute in its obligation, and not at all dependent on the fact of their being duly and lawfully elected. To enforce the Constitution must be accomplished without reference to the consent of any part of the people. Hence it would be a duty to impose upon these States by force the particular governments which, by the supposition, are constitutionally necessary for the execution of the provisions of the Constitution.

It is, on the other hand, quite evident that the enforcement of the constitutional amendments has no connection whatever with the question in debate. The guarantees contained in those provisions rest for their enforcement upon laws passed or to be passed by Congress. Those laws operate upon individual citizens and not upon State governments. They are to be executed by civil process, and not by military force, except where the latter is lawfully called in aid to enforce the precepts of courts of justice. The President, as Chief Executive, is charged, under the Constitution, to see that all these laws be faithfully executed. There is no shadow of reason from any experience of the past to doubt that he will, in the least degree, shrink from the performance of this duty whenever called to its performance. Fortunately, no occasion has yet arisen which has made necessary any such action on his part. There are some who, in their unreasoning opposition, have cited the shocking murder of the Chisholms, in Mississippi, as though the President were in some way responsible for its occurrence or bound to punish it. This is the incapable logic of mere prejudice. It would be quite as reasonable to charge him with responsibility for every murder and mob throughout the country.

But in trying the President on the charge of infidelity to his party principles and pledges, his letter accepting the

Republican nomination must not be overlooked; for he
was supported and elected quite as much upon its terms as
by reason of anything in the platform. This is specially
pertinent to the present discussion, because his letter covers
its ground, while the platform does not touch it. His language on this topic is memorable. He said :

"The resolution of the Convention on the subject of the
permanent pacification of the country and the complete
protection of all its citizens in the free enjoyment of their
constitutional rights, is timely and of great importance.
The condition of the Southern States attracts the attention
and commands the sympathy of the people of the whole
Union. In their progressive recovery from the effects of
the war, *their first necessity is an intelligent and honest administration of government*, which shall protect all classes of
citizens in all their political and private rights. What the
South most needs is peace, and peace depends upon the supremacy of law. There can be no enduring peace if the
constitutional rights of any portion of the people are habitually disregarded. *A division of political parties resting
merely upon the distinction of race, or upon sectional lines, is
always unfortunate and may be disastrous.* The welfare of
the South, alike with that of every other part of the country, depends upon the attractions it can offer to labor, to
immigration, and to capital. But laborers will not go, and
capital will not be ventured, where the Constitution and
the law are set at defiance, and distraction, apprehension,
and alarm take the place of peace-loving and law-abiding
social life. All parts of the Constitution are sacred, and
must be sacredly observed ; the parts that are new, no less
than the parts that are old. The moral and material prosperity of the Southern States can be most effectually ad-
vanced by a hearty and generous recognition of the rights
of all by all—a recognition without reserve or exception.
*With such a recognition fully accorded, it will be practical to
promote, by the influence of all the legitimate agencies of the
general government, the efforts of the people of those States to
obtain for themselves the blessings of honest and capable local
government. If elected, I shall consider it not only my duty,*

*but it will be my ardent desire, to labor for the attainment of
this end.* Let me assure my countrymen of the Southern
States that if I should be charged with the duty of organ-
izing an administration, it will be one which will regard
and cherish their truest interests—the interests of the white
and the colored people, both and equally, and *which will
put forth its best efforts in behalf of a civil policy which will
wipe out forever the distinction between North and South in our
common country.*"

No one, in the light of the circumstances of the situation,
can fail to understand and appreciate the force and meaning of these declarations. The language can neither be
misunderstood nor perverted, and it is not necessary to
look between the lines for a key to their translation. So
far from being chargeable with unfaithfulness to his
pledges as a candidate, the real grievance, which for shame
hides itself, but simulates the form of indignation at the
violation of plighted faith, is that Gen. Hayes meant what
he said, and has been true to his word ; that, as President,
he has redeemed the promises which, as candidate, he made,
not merely to his supporters, but to the country. He has
honorably fulfilled the pledges of his party fealty. He
has done what he could to secure to the people of the Southern States *an intelligent and honest administration of government.* He has done what he could to break up *the division
of political parties resting merely upon the distinctions of race
or upon sectional lines ;* he has done what he could to secure,
by the pledged and promised voluntary co-operation of the
whole community, given by public and representative men,
a recognition of the rights of all, by all ; he has done what
he could, on the basis of that recognition, practically to
promote, by the influence of all the legitimate agencies of
the general government, the efforts of the people of those
States to obtain for themselves the blessings of honest and
capable local government ; he has done what he could, by
putting forth his best efforts in behalf of a civil policy
which will wipe out forever the distinction between North
and South in our common country. Whoever else may
fail hereafter in keeping promises and redeeming pledges,

at least the conscience of the President is clear. He has done exactly what, believing it to be his duty, he pledged himself to do.

But it is said that the President owed it, as a debt of personal and political gratitude to Mr. Packard and the Republicans of Louisiana to maintain his government. Strange idea, this, of political and official obligation! What moral basis is there for such a feeling? It proceeds upon the assumption that party interests are paramount to patriotic duties—that to pay for political and party service is a higher obligation than to obey the Constitution—that a President may exchange, as an equivalent, the peace and prosperity of a whole community for aid rendered in his election by his adherents. This might have answered in the days of robber barons in the feudal ages, but now he serves his party best who best serves his country.

Neither is it true, in any sense, that the President has betrayed the Republican party of the Southern States into the hands of its political enemies, or deserted the just defense of the political and personal rights of any of their citizens. Most assuredly such was not the intent of his policy; neither do I believe such will be its effect.

It may be that, for a time, the Republican party in those States will be disheartened and disorganized by its failure to maintain its power in the government of the State; but there is no reason to believe that that disorganization will result in its permanent dissolution. If it does, it simply proves its own want of an inherent vitalizing force. Activity that can be kept in motion only by galvanic force, is not life, but only a ghastly semblance of it. A party organization that falls to pieces and dissolves immediately on a failure to get or keep possession of office, is not a wholesome organization, and deserves to die. It lives only by the cohesive power of public plunder.

I think better of the Republican party in the Southern States. I see no reason why it should not revive, even Phœnix-like, out of its own ashes, with stronger pinions and loftier flight.

The future of political parties in the United States is, of

course, not matter of knowledge, but of speculation. We can only conjecture the probable course of events, based on our past experience and what we have learned from history and consciousness of the springs and motives of human action. The predictions of the wisest, as well as the most fearful, may come to naught; and yet, because we have no absolute certainty of the stability of nature, no man is considered a fool, who, seeing the sun sink into the night, ventures the reassuring prophecy that it will rise and bring back the day again on the morrow. So, while parties rise and fall, appear and disappear, organize and dissolve, put away old names and put on new, take up new questions and issues and change sides on old ones, still we shall find in this, as the necessity of all free countries, political sentiment dividing the people, at least, into two great party divisions. And so, we have the right to conclude, it will continue to be, even as it is in our days, and was in the days of our fathers.

That the line of division will not be sectional, is certainly greatly to be desired; and I think there is good reason to hope it will not be so. As long as slavery existed, sectional parties were inevitable. As the South became unanimous in the assertion of its claims, the North grew to be unanimous in its opposition. The conflict, in the language of Mr. Seward, was irrepressible; and it was impossible, as Mr. Lincoln clearly announced, for the States long to maintain a Union, half slave and half free. They would have to be either all slave or all free. But the abolition of slavery has removed the only ground of sectional politics. Some of the effects of the institution still remain, and time alone will suffice entirely to remove them. But there is nothing in the character of the people that necessarily creates sectional political differences. The remembrances of civil war, so far as they recall any of its hostilities, are fading under the softening and charity-begetting influence of time, and the friendly intercourse of society and business. There doubtless are and will be some measures and questions, growing out of the events of the Rebellion, that may for a time bind together politically the people of the South; but they must be met, if presented, upon their merits, and decided upon principle; and will not form, in my judgment, the source of permanent or dangerous political agitation. The color line will be effaced in the politics of the South; and the same national questions that divide opinion in the North, will create parties there. Questions of state policy and local administration will constantly arise, and seeking the means of settlement in party debates, will tend further to develop the spirit of party rivalry. Personal ambitions will promote the irresistible tendency; and we shall not have to wait for many elections, before we shall see the contention of party politics establishing its array of partisans in every State, and developing national parties, with their allied State organizations, complete and homogeneous, covering the whole field of political discussion, irrespective of State lines. The colored freedman, as an irritating cause of sectional difference, will then have disappeared from his abnormal position in politics and taken his true though less conspicuous place. The divisions of the white man will be his opportunity. His vote, instead of being repelled, will be solicited by opposing parties, who will, at least each for its own sake, unite in protecting him. His instinct at first will guide him in the exercise of his franchise by the sense of his immediate and personal interest. His experience of party management will be the means of his political education, and enable him to take such part in political movements as he may develope capacity to fill. At least his personal and political rights will be secured, and with them the enactment and administration of laws which will protect him in the just fruits of his labor, and give him that social and political status to which he shall be entitled. Thus will he be enabled to work out his own salvation, if need be, with fear and trembling, but without doubt as to its accomplishment; and all the better for him that it will be his own work. The law struck off the shackles of his bondage and he ceased to be a slave; it conferred upon him the right to vote, and he became a citizen; but to be a man, in the highest and best sense—a man among men—that must be wrought *in* him, and not *upon* him. It is in his case, as in the case of all other races and individuals, the work of general intellectual and moral forces building up the fabric of independent and self-relying character. This is the essential condition, as well as the characteristic function, of political self-government. Taking the view which I have presented of the constitutional and legal grounds of the President's course, and the probable effects of his policy, I defend his Southern policy, not because it was inevitable, but because it was right. Nor do I deem it necessary to apologize for him by shifting the responsibility upon his distinguished predecessor. I do not believe that President Grant ought to have recognized and sustained by force the claims of Packard, while the decision of the Congress, by means of the Electoral Commission, upon the questions arising upon the Louisiana vote, was in suspense. And after that decision was made, I do not think he is to be censured for remitting the question of future executive action to his successor. It is enough to know that President Grant would have done what President Hayes did, but neither is responsible for what the other did or omitted. For one, I am happy to believe that both were right, and are alike entitled to the plaudit of—Well done, good and faithful servants. That such will be the ultimate verdict of the American people and of history, I have no doubt.

CIVIL SERVICE REFORM.

The fifth article of the declaration of principles, announced by the National Republican Convention, at Cincinnati, in 1876, formally committed the Republican party to a Reform of the Civil Service. It is as follows :

" *Fifth.* Under the Constitution, the President and heads of departments are to make nominations for office, the Senate is to advise and consent to appointments, and the House of Representatives is to accuse and prosecute faithless officers. The best interest of the public service demands that these distinctions be respected ; that Senators and Representatives, who may be judges and accusers, should not dictate appointment to office. The invariable rule in appointments should have reference to the honesty, fidelity, and capacity of the appointees, giving to the party in power their places where harmony and vigor of administration require its policy to be represented, but permitting all others to be filled by persons selected with sole reference to the efficiency of the public service and the right of all citizens to share in the honor of rendering faithful service to the country."

The principles distinctly announced in this formula of doctrine may be separately stated as follows :

1. That the spirit of the Constitution requires that, in nominations to office, the Executive Department should act independently of Senators and Representatives ; and that the interests of the service require this independence to be protected against the dictation of members of Congress.

2. That while honesty, fidelity, and capacity should be necessary qualifications in all cases, political considerations should be regarded in appointments to offices whose administration is affected by the decision of political questions.

3. That appointments to other offices should be made solely on the basis of efficiency in the service, and should be non-partisan in their character.

General Hayes, in his letter of acceptance, commented at some length on this declaration. He said :

" The fifth resolution adopted by the Convention is of paramount interest. More than forty years ago, a system of making appointments to office grew up, based on the maxim, · To the victors belong the spoils.' The old rule, the true rule, that honesty, capacity, and fidelity constitute the only real qualification for office, and that there is no other claim, gave place to the idea that party services were to be chiefly considered. All parties, in practice, have adopted this system. It has been essentially modified since its first introduction. It has not, however, been improved. At first, the President, either directly or through the heads of departments, made all the appointments, but gradually the appointing power, in many cases, passed into the control of members of Congress. The offices, in these cases, have become, not merely rewards for party services, but rewards for services to party leaders. This system destroys the independence of the separate departments of the government. It tends directly to extravagance and official incapacity. It is a temptation to dishonesty, it hinders and impairs that careful supervision and strict accountability by which alone faithful and efficient public service can be secured. It obstructs the prompt removal and sure punishment of the unworthy. In every way it degrades the civil service and the character of the government. It is felt, I am confident, by a large majority of the members of Congress to be an intolerable burden and an unwarrantable hindrance to the proper discharge of their legitimate duties. It ought to be abolished. The reform should be thorough, radical, and complete. We should return to the principles and practice of the founders of the government, supplying by legislation, when needed, that which was formerly the established custom. They neither expected nor desired from the public officer any partisan service. They meant that public officers should owe their whole services to the government and to the people. They meant that the officer should be secure in his tenure as long as his personal character remained untarnished and the performance of his duties satisfactory. If elected, I shall conduct the administration of the government upon these principles, and all the constitutional powers vested in the Executive will be employed to establish this reform."

It is impossible to add to the force of this exposure of the evil to be remedied and to the clearness of the explanation of the nature of the remedy. The success of any attempt to carry into effect the principles of this reform will depend much upon the character of the person who, at the time, wields the executive power, but it is manifest that the preliminary step toward its introduction is to affix to the tenure of the Presidential office the disability of a reelection, in order to remove, not only all temptation to abuse its patronage for his personal ends, but, what is almost of equal importance, to take away the very suspicion of it.

Accordingly, with a true insight into the inherent difficulty of the undertaking, General Hayes, in his letter accepting the nomination to the Presidency, as a necessary part of the reform to which he was pledged, took on himself the voluntary vow of ineligibility. He said :

" The declaration of principles by the Cincinnati Convention makes no announcement, in form, of a single Presidential term. I do not assume to add to that declaration ; but, believing that the restoration of the Civil Service to the system established by Washington and followed by the early Presidents, can be best accomplished by an Executive who is under no temptation to use the patronage of his office to promote his own re-election, I desire to perform what I regard as a duty in stating my inflexible purpose, if elected, not to be a candidate for election to a second term."

The first effective step, in my opinion, in a permanent Civil Service reform, is to incorporate that resolution into a Constitutional amendment, limiting the tenure of the Presidential office to a single term. Without that we shall have no guarantee of disinterestedness in the very head of the Civil Service ; and the example of selfish abuse of the public trust, in that high and conspicuous place, will sooner or later infect every department and branch. The removal of the temptation destroys every motive of ambition except to promote the public good, and inspires every official influence with the purity of its source.

By way of inaugurating this reform, the President has issued an executive order, in the following terms :

" No officer should be required or permitted to take part in the management of political organizations, caucuses, conventions, or election campaigns. Their right to vote and to express their views on public questions, either orally or through the press, is not denied, provided it does not interfere with the discharge of their official duties. No assessment for political purposes on officers or subordinates should be allowed." The rule is made applicable to every department of the Civil Service, and every officer of the general government is expected to conform his conduct to its requirements.

An innovation, so great as this, upon the long continued customs of party management, it may be expected, will be received at first, not without doubt and misgiving, as to its practicability and its beneficial results. Many no doubt regard the whole scheme as a Quixotic attempt to correct an imaginary evil; while others look upon it as impracticable and mischievous. It is said that it is useless to attempt, in this way, to divorce the actual administration of the government from active alliance with the support and direction of party politics; and that to do so, is contrary to the spirit of our political institutions, and subversive of popular government through the agency of parties.

But a moment's reflection, it seems to me, suffices to show that this can not be so. If the possession of office and the use and influence of official patronage is necessary to the maintenance of party organizations, what sustains the party in opposition? It may be answered, in that case, not the present, but the hope of future enjoyment keeps the opposition alive. This, under our system, no doubt, is the source of much political activity and strife, but it is certainly not complimentary to the public spirit, intelligence, and patriotism of the body of the people, to assume that their party zeal is simply a hungry hunt for office. If such were the fact, it would only be the stronger proof of the necessity of elevating and purifying our politics.

It is because the proper work of the people has so long been done for them by their self-constituted leaders that it seems to be thought they either never had or have lost the faculty of acting for themselves. A limb grows numb for want of use, and we say we can not use it because it is numb. When the idea was first broached of severing the State from the support of the Church, it was believed by many good people that religion would decay if left to the voluntary support of its votaries. The result showed that, when left to its own resources, its very dependence upon individual and personal effort evoked the enthusiasm necessary to meet the exigency. So the management of party conventions and elections, the choice of delegates, the selection of candidates, the expression of political opinions and framing and shaping party policy is, above all, the business of the people in their primary, voluntary, party associations, free from any official suggestions, dictation, or control. To preserve this supremacy is of the very essence of representative government; the people must assert their mastery, or their servants will become their lords. If the people do not value their right and appreciate their privilege, if they neglect or refuse to devote to this, their own and the greatest public business, the necessary time, oversight, personal attention and participation and money, successfully to conduct it to its legitimate and successful issue, then, to that extent, democratic institutions become inert and fail. The whole conduct of politics will fall into the hands of those who will consider themselves justified by their monopoly in turning it to their own and not the profit of the public.

We do not find, however, in other spheres of voluntary associated action any such weakness in the character of our people. The number of voluntary associations for society, for business, for amusement, for instruction, for charity, for mutual aid, in sickness and in health, for purposes connected with religion, coupled with the intelligent appreciation of political questions pervading all classes of the community, and the prevalent fondness for political discussion, the cheapness and number of newspapers, devoted largely to the spread of political news and ideas, and the habit of making and hearing public speeches on political topics, certainly furnish the most ample guarantees that political parties will not die of inanition, even if they ceased to be fed from the public cribs.

If anything were needed to commend to the American people the idea of a complete and effectual separation of official influence from the free expression of political opinion and feeling, through the voluntary action of parties organized by the people, we shall find it in the spectacle now presented in the so-called Republic of France. There we see the striking example of a contrast. There the

President, Marshal McMahon, dissolved the legislative body of Representatives of the People, because he chose to believe their political opinions were heretical and dangerous. And, although that dissolution could only constitutionally take place, in order to make a renewed appeal, in a new election, to the will of the people, to be expressed through universal suffrage, instead of submitting that appeal to the people, impartially and without the bias from official coercion, he turns the whole combined official machinery of the government into an open and powerful electioneering agency for avowed government candidates. Every one can see what a satire it is upon the freedom of the representative principle. And yet that is just the possibility, which, when the habit of political independence on the part of the people is destroyed here by disuse, that the Civil Service Reform is instituted to avert. The Administration voluntarily offers to the people, and urges upon their acceptance, the right, uninfluenced and unconstrained by official interference, to control the whole machinery of party government. Let them beware, lest, from inertia, rejecting their opportunity, they seek hereafter to reclaim their rights when it is too late to regain them. Let them learn a lesson from the fable. King Log is better than King Stork.

It is no doubt perfectly true that the present stage of the proposed Reform of the Civil Service is quite unsatisfactory; that it needs to be matured and developed; that time and experience are needed to make it definite, and to educate public opinion and official habit to its hearty recognition and acceptance. Nevertheless much has been done simply by making a beginning; for it is perhaps one of those cases in which, while it is the first step that costs the most effort, it also achieves substantially the complete result.

Much too, perhaps, remains to be supplied by legislation. For one, I should hail with satisfaction the enactment of a law which should make it illegal for any member of Congress to solicit or recommend an appointment to Federal office, unless in answer to official inquiry; a law which at least could be pleaded in bar of the importunities to enlist his supposed influence, which, whether to resist or gratify, is an intolerable burden. Then, too, something may be done in diminishing the amount of the Executive patronage; as in case of Marshals of the United States, by lodging the power of appointment in the Courts, whose ministerial officers they are, as has always been the case in regard to their clerks; and, as has been suggested by others, by providing for the nomination of Postmasters by local authority, representing the community for whose benefit this service is specially designed. And in many extensive departments of the public service, including the entire fixed clerical force employed in the Executive business at the National Capital, the Consular service, the Revenue service, both Customs and Internal, the principle might be introduced of indefinite tenures, and appointments, in all but the lowest grade, only by way of promotion. By these and other means, as the experience of others and our own may suggest, we can gradually, but ultimately, establish the Civil Service of the Government, except as to offices whose administration is affected by the general policy of the political party, upon a basis of efficiency, equal to that of our Military and Naval establishments, and purify the politics of the Nation from at least a portion of the corrupt taint communicated by the prevalent lust for office.

THE SILVER QUESTION.

The Republican Convention at Cleveland, upon the question of restoring silver to its place in our coinage, expressed itself in the following resolution:

" *Resolved*, That we are in favor of both silver and gold as money; that both shall be a legal tender for the payment of all debts, except where otherwise specially provided by law, with coinage and valuation so regulated, that our people shall not be placed at a disadvantage in our trade with foreign nations, and that both metals shall be kept in circulation as the money of the nation, as contemplated by the Constitution; and we therefore demand the remonetization of silver."

This is a very distinct declaration in favor of the re-establishment of the bi-metallic standard, and of the restoration of silver, not as a subsidiary coinage, but on an equal footing with gold, as a legal tender, in payment of all debts, and in all sums, except where the law otherwise specially provides. The only conditions to its remonetization are, that the coinage and the valuation shall be so regulated that we shall not suffer in our foreign trade, and that both metals shall be kept in circulation together at home. This qualification as to the coinage is undoubtedly necessary and proper. In the present relation between the market value of gold and silver bullion, it would be out of the question to permit the free coinage of silver on private account. The coinage of silver should, for the present, be made on government account alone, and in quantities which would not prevent the circulation of gold. The single and simple limitation upon the amount coined will be ample for this purpose. This would be merely following the example of the Latin Union, the members of which, by restricting the quantum of their annual coinage of silver, have counteracted the policy of Germany in demonetizing silver, and prevented the loss by export of their gold. The same principle is illustrated by our subsidiary coin, which, although depreciated below the standard value of our own silver bullion, nevertheless is kept in circulation by a demand. which the government preserves by avoiding an excess in issue. The only limit as to coinage, therefore, is to keep it in the control of the government, so as not to issue it faster, or in greater quantities, than it can be absorbed in the circulation by the legitimate demands for its use. No regulation is needed in respect to the ratio of valuation between gold and silver, except to adhere, for the present, to that heretofore known to our laws, namely, one to about sixteen. This is more conservative than the valuation established in other countries, where both metals are used, and in the present condition of affairs, gives us an advantage, in respect to the object proposed, of preserving both metals in our circulation. Under the influence of the restricted coinage of silver in France, where the ratio of silver to gold is fifteen and one-half to one, gold continues to circulate on an equal footing with silver, without being driven out by the cheaper metal. Of course, a similar result in this country is more certainly assured by a valuation, according to which gold is rated higher in its silver value than in France. If in that country, where gold only commands fifteen and a half times its weight in silver, it is not found profitable to export it to other countries, then there will be no danger of its exportation from this country, where it will command sixteen times its weight in silver. The tendency, on the contrary, would be, for our silver to flow to France, and other silver-using countries, in exchange for their gold, which we valued at a higher price; a tendency, however, as already stated, which those countries counteract by limiting the amount of their silver coinage.

All the conditions, then, prescribed by the Republican resolution for the remonetization of silver will be adequately fulfilled by the restoration to our coinage and currency of the ancient silver dollar, on government account alone, and under the control of the government as to the rapidity and quantity of the actual coinage. As the capacity of our mints is limited to an annual coinage, as is said, of less than fifty millions, before any excess could be put in circulation the tendency and effect of the new silver currency would be ascertained from actual experience, and developed evils corrected by necessary legislation.

There seems to be in the resolution of the Republican Convention an implication that there may possibly be existing special legislation which would forbid silver, when restored, from being a legal tender in all cases. An examination of our legislation will show that there is no ground for any such intimation.

The facts of our legislation, affecting this point, are not susceptible of dispute. The original coinage act, of April 2, 1792. established the dollar, or unit, to be of the value of a Spanish milled dollar, as then current, and to contain 371,4 grains of pure silver, the proportional value of gold to silver in all cases, current as money, being fixed as fifteen to one. This continued in force until the coinage act of January 18, 1837, when the ratio of value between gold and silver was changed to a proportion of about sixteen to one, by changing the quantity of pure gold in the gold coins, but leaving the quantity of pure silver in the dollar precisely as it always before had been. The weight of the coined silver dollar was reduced from 416 grains of standard silver to 412½ ; but this was effected by changing the amount of alloy alone. On the other hand, the gold unit, or dollar, of 1792 contained twenty-four seventy-five hundredth grains of pure gold, while that of 1837 consisted only of twenty-three twenty-two hundredths of pure gold. Gold, in other words, had been undervalued in the original ratio ; and it was reduced in quantity in proportion to silver by the new regulations of 1837. But the silver dollar remained precisely the same, and was a legal tender according to its nominal value for any sums whatever.

This continued to be the law until the coinage act of February 12, 1873, and that did not alter the legal quality of the original silver dollar. It indeed, declared that the one dollar gold piece of the standard weight of twenty-five eight-tenth grains, but containing the previously established quantity of pure gold, namely, twenty-three twenty-two hundredth grains, should be the unit of value ; and it provided that the silver coins of the United States should be —a trade dollar, a half dollar, a quarter dollar, and a dime ; the trade dollar weighing 420 grains of standard silver, but 378 grains of pure silver, being 6¾ grains more than was contained in the old silver dollar ; and this trade dollar, with the other named silver coins, was declared to be a legal tender for amounts not exceeding five dollars in one payment. But nothing was said as to the original silver dollar, and it was left, so far as the law was concerned, where it stood before. Its complete and final demonetization is due to a section of the Revised Statutes (see. 3516), which prohibited the future issue from the mint of any coins other than those specifically enumerated, the old silver dollar having been dropped from the list, and sec. 3586, which limits the legal tender quality of all silver coins to the amount of five dollars.

There is no claim made, that prior to March 18, 1869, any of the obligations of the government were by law specially payable in gold. On the contrary, until that time, the question was whether, by the terms of the law creating them, they were not payable in legal-tender paper money or greenbacks. To settle that question Congress passed the act of that date, " to strengthen the public credit." It was thereby provided and declared, in order to remove any doubt as to the purpose of the government to discharge all just obligations to the public creditors, and to settle conflicting questions and interpretations of the laws by virtue of which such obligations had been contracted, that the faith of the United States was thereby solemnly pledged to the payment *in coin*, or its equivalent, of all the obligations of the United States not bearing interest, known as the United States notes, and of all the interest-bearing obligations of the United States, except in cases where the law authorizing the issue of such obligations had expressly provided that the same might be paid in lawful money or other currency *than gold and silver*. As none of these obligations were, by the law creating them, made expressly payable in other currency than gold and silver, this pledge applied to the entire public debt as then outstanding. The same act of Congress also solemnly pledged the faith of the United States to make provision, at the earliest practicable period, for the redemption of the United States notes *in coin*.

It will be observed that in this act the pledge is to pay in coin, and coin is used as meaning gold and silver.

The funding act of July 14, 1870, provides for the issue of the bonds bearing interest at 5, 4½, and 4 per cent., the aggregate amount of 1,500 millions, for the purpose of retiring and funding the 5–20 bonds, so-called, which bore a higher rate of interest. The bonds authorized to be issued for that purpose were expressly made " redeemable *in coin of the present standard value*," and " bearing interest, payable semi-annually, *in such coin*."

The Specie Resumption Act, of January 14, 1875, declares "that on and after the 1st day of January, A. D. 1879, the Secretary of the Treasury shall, redeem, *in coin*, the United States legal-tender notes then outstanding, on their presentation for redemption at the office of the Assistant-Treasurer of the United States, in the city of New York, in sums not less than $50. And to enable the Secretary of the Treasury to prepare and provide for the redemption in this act authorized or required, he is authorized to use any surplus revenues, from time to time in the Treasury, not otherwise appropriated, and to issue, sell, and dispose of, at not less than *par in coin*, either of the description of bonds of the United States, described in the act of Congress approved July 14, 1870, entitled "An Act to authorize the Refunding of the National Debt," with like privileges and exceptions, to the extent necessary to carry this act into effect, and to use the proceeds thereof for the purposes aforesaid."

So that the bonds authorized to be issued under this act are, like those authorized by the Funding Act of July 14, 1870, to be redeemable *in coin of the standard value of that date.*

The fact, then, clearly appears that no part of the public debt of the United States, by virtue of any special provisions of law under which it was contracted, is payable otherwise than in coin, consisting of gold and silver of the standard value, as established by law in force on the 14th day of July, 1870. As on that date the silver dollar, containing 371¼ grains of pure silver—the ancient silver dollar, the dollar of the fathers—was a lawful coin of the United States, of standard value, and a legal tender in all sums for the payment of all debts, equally with coins of gold, the conclusion is irresistible that the United States have to-day the legal right to pay every part of its debt, principal and interest, as it becomes due, in coins of that description; and, if they can not otherwise be procured, to purchase in the open market silver bullion, at any price, no matter how cheap, and coin that description of silver dollars in any amounts needed for that purpose.

The question of legal right being disposed of in that way,

disposes of the question of moral right in the same way.
It does not, of course, always happen that legal and moral
right coincide. But here it is a question of good faith, and
we have already seen that the only faith expressly pledged
was to pay in coin, of gold or silver, of the then current
standard value. No implication can be raised where the
contract is express, and it does not alter the case to say
that, in point of fact, no silver coins were in circulation and
the coinage had long before ceased. Gold coins were not
in general circulation either; but what is more to the
point, and quite conclusive, is, that the right and option to
coin silver dollars and use them in payment of debts, was
at the time undiminished. The silver dollar was a lawful
coin, a legal tender, and the government, neither expressly
nor by any implication, gave any pledge not to resume its
coinage and use it in payment. Any opinion to the contrary, that it would not be done, was individual merely—
nothing but a personal conjecture—and not binding on the
public authority. The law itself was notice to the world
of the continued existence of the right; and no one had
any ground to presume that the government would not restore silver to its currency in lawful payment of its obligations whenever considerations of public policy, which
are merely motives of public interest, should incline it so
to do.

There is nothing, then, to prevent the restoration of the
silver dollar to its place in our currency, as an unlimited
legal tender, so far as payment of the public creditor
is concerned, except considerations of expediency. If to
do so would depreciate the public credit, lower the market
value of the four per cent. bonds, and interfere materially
with the process of refunding the public debt at a lower rate
of interest—in other words, if it shall appear to be in the
public interest to pay the principal and interest of the
bonds in gold, then, clearly, it ought to be done; but not
otherwise; and if it is to be done, let it be said by authority of law, which all will understand and respect.

It seems to be thought by some, that as gold has been
exacted by the Treasury in payment of the bonds issued

under the act of July 14, 1870, that that imposed upon the
government the obligation to construe the contract as an
obligation to repay interest and principal in gold. But
that circumstance can not affect the construction of the
law, although it may establish an equity in favor of its
modification. The same appeal, however, was not entertained when it was urged in favor of paying the five-
twenties in greenbacks, that that was the currency in which
they had been purchased.

But the question of remonetizing silver is altogether distinct from the question in what coin the public debt ought
to be paid ; and each must be decided, as every other public question, independently, on its own merits, and upon its
own public policy. If we remonetized silver, we can still
pay our bonds in gold, if we are bound to do so, or if, without an obligation, we still see fit to do so, for any sufficient
reason ; and if, by remonetizing silver, we make it easier
and cheaper to pay in gold, certainly those who claim the
right to be paid in gold have no right to object.

That such will be the effect is my firm conviction, and it
furnishes the controlling reason why we should restore to
our coinage and currency the silver dollar as proposed.

It seems to be assumed throughout, as an indisputable
proposition, by the opponents of the silver restoration, that
its remonetization will have the effect merely to drive away
the gold coin, without increasing the value of silver ; that
the present difference in value between gold and silver bullion will be maintained after the remonetization of silver
has been effected. And this is based upon the further assumption, that that present difference is based upon a permanent depreciation in the value of silver, in consequence
of the large increase of its recent annual production from
our mines.

This assumption leaves out of the account entirely, as
circumstances of no significance, the demonetization of
silver in the German empire, the consequent restriction of
its coinage by the Latin Union, the demonetization of silver in this country, and the financial derangements that
have prevented its usual export to India ; all which have

conspired simultaneously to diminish the demand for it, at the very time when the supply was largely increased.

The effect of remonetizing silver fully may be inferred from the influence already exerted by the introduction into our coinage of the comparatively small amounts needed for subsidiary coins. It is stated by the report made to the House of Commons, by the select committee of which Mr. Goschen was chairman, in July, 1876, that the latest increase in the new mines in this country had not thrown any additional supplies of silver on the European markets; that the cause of the diminished export of silver, notwithstanding the increased production, is to be sought in the coining operations of the United States government, and is due, in the main, to an act passed for substituting silver coin for the paper "fractional currency." And in speaking of the effect of the demonetization of silver upon its exchangeable value as a commodity, the same report says "that it is obvious that if effect should be given to the policy of substituting gold for silver, wherever it is feasible, and giving gold, for the sake of its advantages in international commerce, the preference even among populations whose habits and customs are in favor of silver, and thus displacing silver from the position (which it has always occupied) of doing the work of the currency over at least as large an area as gold, no possible limits can be assigned to the further fall in its value which would inevitably take place." It is equally obvious that a contrary policy would have a contrary effect. And Mr. Walter Bagehot, one of the best authorities on such a subject in England, writing in April, 1877, said: "I consider that the rise in the price of silver, from 47*d*. last summer to 55½*d*. now, shows the preceding great fall from 54½*d*. last February, to be only a momentary accident in a new and weak market, *and not the permanent effect of lasting causes.*" (Preface to Depreciation of Silver.) And elsewhere, contrasting the prices of gold and silver, he states explicitly that "there is no evidence whatever that general prices in any country where prices are measured in silver, have risen in any such ratio;" in other words, that silver has not fallen, but gold has risen, in proportion to the average general prices of other commodities. And the same writer, speaking expressly of the effect of bringing silver again into use as a currency in this country, says:

"If they (the United States) did, it is certain that the price in silver would for the moment rise, because so very large an extra quantity would at once be required, and it is very possible that this price might not again fall. The final regulation of the price of silver is the cost at which it can be produced in the least fertile mine that can maintain itself in working. At the present moment there are new mines as to whose extent there are very various accounts, which may supersede some of the worst of those at work, and so lessen the maximum cost of the production of silver—the cost which fixes its price. But if so large a new demand for silver as that for supplying the United States with money were added to the existing demands, very possibly the extra fertility of these new mines might be exhausted before that demand was satisfied. These new mines might come to be not so much better than the old ones as to throw any old mine out of work; *and if so, the price of silver would remain what it formerly was. And if this happened, silver would be as good a standard of value as it has ever been.*"

And in this country Mr. David A. Wells, writing against the proposal to restore silver to the currency, took pains to remove the supposed argument in its favor, based on the cheapness of such currency, by showing that its necessary effect would be to equalize its value with that of gold.

That is precisely the reason why the measure should be adopted, because it would raise the price of silver in terms of gold, by reducing the price of gold, and bringing both coins ultimately to the same par. In this way no injustice would be done to the public creditor, whom, then, it would be as easy to pay in gold as silver; and the silver added to the circulation would be equal to an accumulation of that amount of gold. In the double coin the transition could more easily be made, by which our paper currency would be convertible at par into either coin; and the great injustice, hardship, and bankruptcy involved in requiring private contracts, made in a currency of irredeemable paper, to be performed in gold, and the value of that gold greatly enhanced by giving it a monopoly of the currency, would be averted.

I join, therefore, heartily in the demand for the remonetization of silver—the restoration to our coinage and currency of the ancient silver dollar—without other limit than is secured by government control of its quantity, guided by an experience of the results. It is equally the demand of justice and sound public policy, the indispensible condition and only safe road to Resumption—a resumption of specie payments which shall not retire and cancel our Treasury Notes, but make them equal in value to silver and gold, and exchangeable at par with coin, on demand—and so preserve and perpetuate them as our National Currency —the cheapest, the most uniform, the perfect American Currency.

www.ingramcontent.com/pod-product-compliance
Lightning Source LLC
Chambersburg PA
CBHW021628270326
41931CB00008B/922